Pig in jeal
MY MOM
IS THE COOLEST
MW01630049

piginjeans.com

Dedicated to
my coolest mom
and my sweetest boys.

Mother's Day is almost here!
Brian is looking for the coolest gift for his coolest mom.

4

"Hi Brian! What are you doing?" Nathan asked.
"I'm looking for the coolest Mother's Day gift for my coolest mom!"
Brian answered.

5

"Wait a minute," Nathan said.
"I thought **MY** mom is the coolest."

"No no no, **MY** mom is the coolest," Brian responded.

MY mom is the coolest!
NO! MY mom is the coolest!

MY mom is the coolest.

MY mom is the coolest!
NO! MY mom is the coolest!

Our mom is the coolest.

Brian began to explain why his mom
is the coolest. "My mom is like my best friend," Brian said.

"She listens to me when I'm happy."

"She listens to me when I'm sad."

"My mom is so cool, she knows the answer to every question," Brian said.

Mom, where are my socks?

On the floor.

Where is the remote?

Behind the couch.

Can I have a snack?

No.

"My mom is my biggest cheerleader," Brian continued.
"She is there at my soccer game."

"She is there at my piano recital."

"You know what else? I think my mom has super powers!" Brian said.
"She always cooks food that I like. It's like she can read my mind! She even
knows that my favorite pizza is cheese pizza from Mike, the pizza guy!"

"My mom can ride her bike super fast."
Whoa!
Oh dear, I can't stop!

"She can do many things at once.
She can work, attend phone meetings and
manage the house, all at the same time!"

"My mom always makes me laugh."
Here, put this underwear on.

You said "UNDERWEAR"!!!!
HAHA!!
HAHA!!

"Wow, your mom is pretty cool," Nathan said.

"But MY mom is super duper cool too!" Nathan explained.
"She reads cool books with me every day, and she knows big words."

"She wakes up super early to prepare breakfast for the family."

"She is always proud of me. She hangs all of my art on the fridge, even the one where I just scribbled with my eyes closed!" Nathan said.

"When I'm sick, she takes care of me," Nathan continued.
"She gives me medicine, makes me soup and gives me hugs.
I would feel better the next day!"

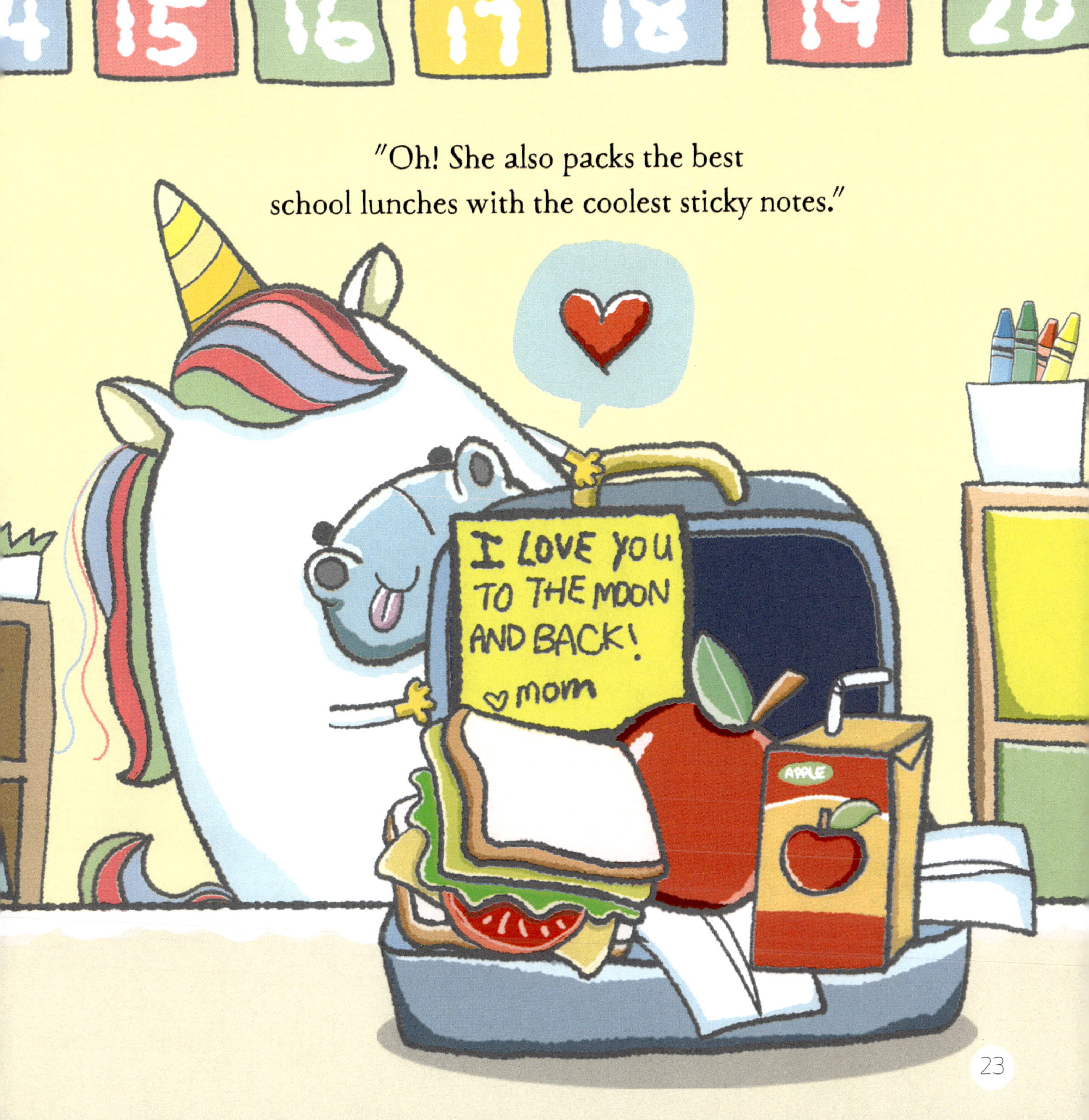

"Oh! She also packs the best
school lunches with the coolest sticky notes."

23

"Wow Nathan, your mom **IS** pretty cool," Brian admitted.
"But MY mom can do the coolest pose!"

"Well, my mom can do the coolest dance!" Nathan said.

After a long discussion of why their moms are so cool,
Brian finally figured out what to do for Mother's Day.
Nathan had an idea too.

Brian folded a piece of paper in half and worked on some art.

Nathan planted some seeds
and watered the plant.

Brian made a very cool Mother's Day card. He drew his mom's favorite cupcake and taped it onto a piece of paper. He even added wacky arms and legs!

Nathan planted a beautiful flower for his mom.
He also added a cool pair of sunglasses!

The boys were so excited to present their gifts.
"HAPPY MOTHER'S DAY TO THE COOLEST MOM EVER!"
they both said.

Brian and Nathan sat down to rest.
"Wait a minute," Brian said. "Who has the coolest mom then?"
"It looks like both our moms are just as cool," Nathan answered.
"So it's a tie?" Brian asked.
"It's a tie," Nathan said.

At the end of the day,
the boys agreed on one thing...

They agreed that all mothers are strong, intelligent, beautiful...

...and the coolest.

 THE END

My dad's the funniest.

Bonus Writing Exercise!

My mom is the coolest because:

1) _______________________________

2) _______________________________

3) _______________________________

The Coolest Word Search!

```
S M O T H E R U
M E S E L O O C
A V S D N I K A
R O O M L A C R
T L B C E L O E
```

MOTHER   KIND
COOL   CALM
LOVE   CARE
SMART   BOSS

FREE COLORING PRINTABLES:
piginjeans.com/freebie

@piginjeans

Follow us on Instagram!

Tag us in a photo of your child or class reading the book
to be featured on our socials!

Made in the USA
Columbia, SC
31 January 2023